Published by Sequoia Children's Publishing,
an imprint of Sequoia Publishing & Media, LLC

Sequoia Publishing & Media, LLC,
a division of Phoenix International Publications, Inc.

8501 West Higgins Road, Chicago, Illinois 60631
34 Seymour Street, London W1H 7JE
Heimhuder Straße 81, 20148 Hamburg

Compilation © 2024 Sequoia Publishing & Media, LLC

You're So Punny!, Silly to Say, Knock, Knock! Who's There? Fun!, Otter This World
© 2022 Sequoia Publishing & Media, LLC

CustomerService@PhoenixInternational.com

Sequoia Children's Publishing and associated logo are trademarks and/or registered trademarks of Sequoia Publishing & Media, LLC.

All rights reserved. This publication may not be reproduced in whole or in part by any means without permission from the copyright owners. Permission is never granted for commercial purposes.

This book is sold subject to the condition that it shall not, by way of trade or otherwise, be lent, resold, hired out, or otherwise circulated without the publisher's prior consent in any form or binding or cover other than that in which it is published and without similar condition being imposed on the subsequent purchaser.

www.SequoiaKidsBooks.com

ISBN: 978-1-64269-435-2

TABLE OF CONTENTS

You're So Punny! 6
Pun-derful Wordplay

Silly to Say 30
Limericks, Tongue Twisters, and Riddles

Knock, Knock! Who's There? Fun! 54

Otter This World 78
Animal Jokes

The Giant Joke Book for Kids

You're So Punny!

Pun-derful Wordplay

Illustrations © Shutterstock 2023 Borbely Edit; hand draw; Iconic Bestiary; Ihor Biliavskyi; kintomo; Klara Viskova; losw; Magicleaf; Masa Marinkovic; mckenna71; MisterEmil; Mochipet; MyClipArtStore.com; Nadezda Barkova; Nadya_Art; owatta; Pogorelova Olga; Pushnova; SKvector; soratoki; svtdesign; Thidarat Suteeratat; tmicons; Tomacco; vectorplus; VectorShots; wowomnom; Yulia M; yum-yum; Pinar Ince (p. 5)

TABLE OF CONTENTS

Pun Time! Fun Time! 8

Lettuce Laugh! 10
Food Puns

Pun-derful People Puns 14

Punny on Purpose 16
General Puns

Silly Billy Jokes 20

Silly Jilly Jokes 24

The Pun Continues 28

PUN TIME! FUN TIME!

You've probably heard a lot of puns without even knowing it. They're a very popular type of joke. Especially with kids!

Sometimes puns make us roll our eyes. They can be so bad, they're good. But usually they make us giggle!

So what is a pun? Puns are jokes that are playful with words! Sometimes puns are jokes that use two words that sound the same but mean different things. Sometimes puns make jokes using words that might have different meanings.

It sounds confusing, right? Here are some jokes that use puns:

Why are teddy bears never hungry?
They are always stuffed!

And...

What do you call a sleeping bull?
A bull-dozer.

This book is full of fun-tastic puns!

LETTUCE LAUGH!
FOOD PUNS

What did the strawberry say to the banana?

"You've got a-peel."

Why did the mushroom go to the party?

Because he was a fungi.

What do you call cheese that doesn't belong to you?

Nacho cheese.

What do you get when you cross a cheetah and a hamburger?

Fast food.

What did one cucumber say to the other cucumber?

"Boy, are we in a pickle."

Why did the cookie go to the doctor?

It felt crummy.

What kind of candy is never on time?

Choco-late.

What do you get when you cross a cow and an earthquake?

A milkshake.

LAFFY TAFFY CANDY PUNS

Laffy Taffy is a candy that is popular because it tastes good! And, because every single candy makes us giggle. Every wrapper of the candy has a joke on it. A lot of the jokes on Laffy Taffy candies use puns to make us laugh.

Here are some punny jokes that appear on Laffy Taffy:

How do bulls write? With a bullpen!

What do cats eat for breakfast? Mice Krispies!

Why shouldn't you tell an egg a joke?
Because it will crack up.

What did the hamburger say to the hot dog?
"Nice to meat you!"

How do you fix a torn lettuce leaf?
With a cabbage patch.

FUNNY FACT

People have been making puns across many different languages for a long, long time! In the Middle East, Palestinians (PAL-ES-TIN-EE-UNS) sometimes say puns to entertain people at weddings. This has happened for hundreds of years.

Why did the banana go to the doctor?
It wasn't peeling well.

Why was the pickle proud?
It was kind of a big dill.

Why did the students eat their homework?
Their teacher told them it was a piece of cake.

What do you get when you cross a cow and a duck?
Milk and quackers.

PUN-DERFUL PEOPLE PUNS

Why did the skiers fall asleep on the mountain?
Because they were snow bored.

Why was Polite Pete unable to finish his puzzle?
Because he hated using cross words.

What has 18 legs and catches flies?
A baseball team.

What time is it when you go to the dentist?
Tooth-hurty.

What is a witch's favorite class in school?
Spelling.

Why do football players go to the bank?
To get their quarterback.

FUNNY FACT

Every year, there's a big pun championship in Austin, Texas. It's like the Super Bowl but for puns. If you wanted to compete, what pun would you use to try to win it all?

Punny on Purpose
General Puns

Why was the math book sad?
Because it had so many problems.

What do you get when you cross a tiger and the beach?
Sandy claws.

Why was the belt arrested?
For holding up the pants.

What do you need to spot an iceberg?
Good ice sight.

What do you get when you cross a snowman and a vampire?
Frostbite.

HEE HEE!

How do you talk to a giant?
Use big words.

What kind of clothing does a house wear?
Address.

Did You Know?

The author William Shakespeare wrote some of the most famous plays in history. Have you ever heard of *Romeo & Juliet* or *Hamlet*?

Want to hear something really silly about Shakespeare? He liked to include puns about poop in his writing. Ew! Gross! But also funny!

Many famous authors love using puns! Lewis Carroll was the author of *Alice's Adventures in Wonderland*. The book is full of puns.

HEE HEE!

Why are stadiums so cold?
Because they are full of fans.

Why is six afraid of seven?
Because seven eight nine.

Where do generals keep their armies?
In their sleevies.

Why did the baseball player go to jail?

For stealing bases.

What kind of tree fits in your hand?

A palm tree.

How do you know the ocean is friendly?

It waves.

Punning Around

Want to learn how to be good at making puns? Just like every skill, all it takes is practice, practice, practice! Can you think up a silly pun right now?

Think of words that sound the same but don't mean the same thing. Practice coming up with puns to share with your friends and your family. Do your jokes make them laugh?

Silly Billy Jokes

What does Silly Billy do to relax?

He sits on the TV and watches the couch.

FUNNY FACT

Silly Billy and Silly Jilly jokes are about imaginary characters named Billy and Jilly who give us giggles! They do a lot of things that don't make a lot of sense. The things they do are so ridiculous, they make us laugh!

Why does Silly Billy always have lots of ice cubes?

To keep the freezer cold.

Why did Silly Billy get stuck at the intersection?

He was waiting for the stop sign to change.

Silly Billy went to see the barber.

"Do you want a haircut?" asked the barber.

"No," said Billy. "I want them all cut."

Why did Silly Billy buy a brown cow?

Because he wanted chocolate milk.

Why did Silly Billy sit on his watch?

He wanted to be on time.

FUNNY FACT

Computers can do a lot, but it's hard to teach a computer to pun! A man named Max Parke created the Punerator, a computer that he tried to teach to pun. It was no match for the punning power of humans!

Why did Silly Billy buy birdseed?
He wanted to grow his own birds.

Why did Silly Billy hop across the street?
Because the sign said, "Don't Walk."

Why was Silly Billy staring at the orange juice container?
Because it said "concentrate."

SILLY JILLY JOKES

Silly Jilly wanted to go to the park, but she saw a sign that said, "Public Park – Left."

So she went back home.

Silly Jilly and her friend both jumped off the high dive at the same time.

Who hit the water first?

Silly Jilly's friend. Silly Jilly had to stop and ask for directions.

What did Silly Jilly name her pet zebra?

Spot.

HA HA HA!

Why did Silly Jilly put her cash in the oven?

Because she heard it was a lot of dough.

Why did Silly Jilly take a mirror with her when she went to the bank?

So she could identify herself.

FUNNY FACT

Ben & Jerry's is famous for using puns in its ice cream flavor names. Funny Ben & Jerry's flavor puns include Americone Dream, and Oat of this Swirled. What makes those two names funny? Can you spot the puns?!

Why did Silly Jilly wear a swimsuit to work?

She had joined a carpool.

Why did Silly Jilly bring a bowling ball to the pet store?

She wanted to see the fish bowl.

FUNNY FACT

With over 171,000 different words being used today, English is a fantastic language for making puns!

Why did Silly Jilly laugh on Monday morning?

She heard a good joke on Friday night.

What did Silly Jilly order for lunch?

A cheeseburger, hold the cheese

Why did Silly Jilly sleep with an inner tube?

Because she had a waterbed.

Why did Silly Jilly eat a dollar bill?

Because her mom said it was for lunch.

THE PUN CONTINUES...

Why did the scientist install a knocker on the front door?
To win the no-bell prize.

What do prisoners use to call each other?
Cell phones.

Why did Silly Billy never eat bananas?
He could never find the zipper.

Why does it take so long to run from second base to third base?
There's a short stop along the way.

What did the skeleton make for dinner?
Spare ribs.

What ingredient does a pirate add to spaghetti?
Garrr-lic.

The Giant Joke Book for Kids

Silly to Say

Limericks, Tongue Twisters, and Riddles

Illustrations © Shutterstock 2023 ayelet-keshet; BeataGFX; brgfx; Chaim Devine; Dmitrieva A; Dmitry Natashin; graphic-line; HappyPictures; iana kauri; johavel; lady-luck; Lebedev Yury; marina.soboleva; Merfin; Mio Buono; MyClipArtStore.com; Olga Utchenko; Pushnova; Sabelskaya; stas11; StockVectorsIllustrations; Sudowoodo; svtdesign; vectorplus

TABLE OF CONTENTS

Limericks, Tongue Twisters, and Riddles...Oh My! 32

Laughable Limericks 34

Terrific Tongue Twisters 42

Riddle Me This! 46

Hilarious Hinky Pinky 50

Head-Scratchers and Hink Pinks 52

LIMERICKS, TONGUE TWISTERS, AND RIDDLES...OH MY!

Sometimes, things are funny because they sound silly when read aloud. And that makes us laugh!

Limericks are five-line poems that always have certain lines that rhyme. In limericks, the first, second, and fifth lines always rhyme with each other. The third and fourth lines rhyme with one another. That makes them sound really hilarious when you say them out loud.

Sometimes, things are hilarious because they are hard to say quickly. Tongue twisters use words back-to-back to make us trip over our tongues. They can make our tongues feel double in size. Don't worry! This feeling is normal when reading tongue twisters.

And sometimes, things are funny because they challenge our brains in fun ways. Riddles are mini games for our minds. Try your best to solve them, and have fun along the way!

Tongue Twister Tips

If you have some trouble reading tongue twisters out loud, it's OK! They are supposed to be tough to read. That's what makes them so silly.

When you read a tongue twister for the first time, read it out loud very slowly. Do this until you are comfortable. Then, try saying it out loud faster. Can you do it?

Keep on practicing!

LAUGHABLE LIMERICKS

Hickory dickory dock.
The mouse ran up the clock.
The clock struck one,
The mouse ran down.
Hickory dickory dock.

There was an old man of Darjeeling
Who boarded a bus bound for Ealing.
It said on the door,
"Don't spit on the floor."
So, he stood up and spat on the ceiling.

Darjeeling is a city in India.
Ealing is a neighborhood in London, England.

There was a young lady named Bright,
Whose speed was much faster than light.
She set off one day
In a relative way,
And returned on the previous night.

There Once Was A...

Many limericks use the names of places to start off the poem.

Then, the best limericks end with a really funny—or surprising—punchline.

Here's a really fun example that does both of these things:

Leeds is a city in England.

> There once was a farmer from Leeds
> Who swallowed a packet of seeds.
> It soon came to pass,
> He was covered in grass,
> But has all the tomatoes he needs.

Do you understand that joke? Did the surprise ending make you laugh?

A tutor who tooted the flute
Tried to teach two young tooters to toot;
Said the two to the tutor,
"Is it harder to toot, or
To tutor two tooters to toot?"

There was an old man who said, "Well!
Will NOBODY answer this bell?
I have pulled day and night,
Till my hair has grown white,
But nobody answers this bell!"

FUNNY FACT

Limericks have been around for more than 300 years!

There was a young lady whose bonnet
Came untied when the birds sat upon it.
But she said, "I don't care!
All the birds in the air
Are welcome to sit on my bonnet!"

> This is a made-up place name. It's hard to find a rhyme for *tiger*!

There was a young lady from Iger
Who smiled as she rode on a tiger.
They returned from the ride
With the lady inside,
And the smile on the face of the tiger.

There was an old man with a beard
Who said, "It is just as I feared!—
Two owls and a hen,
Four larks and a wren,
Have all built their nests in my beard!"

There was a young lady whose eyes
Were unique as to color and size;
When she opened them wide,
People all turned aside,
And started away in surprise.

There was an old man in a boat
Who said, "I'm afloat! I'm afloat!"
When they said, "No! You ain't!"
He was ready to faint,
That unhappy old man in a boat.

There was a young lady whose chin
Resembled the point of a pin;
So she had it made sharp,
And purchased a harp,
And played several tunes with her chin.

Did You Know?

Many famous writers have written limericks. They are a very popular type of poem. Edward Lear wrote more than 100 limericks in *A Book of Nonsense*. This book was written way back in 1846. It helped to make limericks popular. Edward Lear was called the "father of limericks."

Lewis Carroll didn't just pen the punny *Alice's Adventures in Wonderland*—he was known for writing limericks, too!

There was an old man with a nose
Who said, "If you choose to suppose
That my nose is too long,
You are certainly wrong!"
That remarkable man with a nose.

There was an old man of the coast,
Who placidly sat on a post;
But when it was cold,
He relinquished his hold,
And called for some hot buttered toast.

A flea and a fly in a flue
Were imprisoned, so what could they do?
"Let us flee," said the fly.
"Let us fly," said the flea.
So they flew through a flaw in the flue.

HEE HEE!

• Limerick

Funny Fact

Limerick is not just the name of a type of poem. Did you know that Limerick is also the name of one of the biggest cities in Ireland?

TERRIFIC TONGUE TWISTERS

Try saying these tricky phrases three times fast!

A bit of better butter makes a bitter batter better.

Which wristwatches are Swiss wristwatches?

Red leather, yellow leather.

Unique New York.

Synonym for cinnamon.

Three free throws.

Fish sauce shop.

HEE HEE!

Selfish shellfish.

Beef broth.

A nice dish of fresh fish.

How much wood would a woodchuck chuck

If a woodchuck could chuck wood?

A woodchuck would chuck

As much wood as a woodchuck could

If a woodchuck could chuck wood.

FUNNY FACT

The tongue twister that starts, "How much wood would a woodchuck chuck" first appeared in a song from a Broadway musical in the early 1900s!

Now can you say these tongue twisters three times fast?

Many minty myths.

Greek grapes.

Shrink shrimpy sheep.

Walter's walrus walked on water.

Steve stole snow stoves.

Black bug's blood, blue bug's blood.

Which wicked witch wished which wicked wish?

FUNNY FACT

The famous tongue twister that begins, 'She sells seashells' is thought to be written for a famous fossil hunter named Mary Anning.

Peter Piper picked a peck of pickled peppers.

A peck of pickled peppers Peter Piper picked.

If Peter Piper picked a peck of pickled peppers,

Where's the peck of pickled peppers Peter Piper picked?

She sells seashells by the seashore.

The shells she sells are surely seashells.

So if she sells shells on the seashore,

I'm sure she sells seashore shells.

RIDDLE ME THIS!

What goes all over the country but doesn't move?
Roads.

What starts with *P* and ends with *E* and has a million letters in it?
Post office.

What goes up and never comes down?
Your age.

What has five eyes but can't see?
The Mississippi River.

FUNNY FACT

The oldest written riddle is from around 4,000 years ago. It was found in the area that is now the country of Iraq.

What has a mouth, but never talks, and a bed, but never sleeps?
A river.

What goes up the chimney down but not down the chimney up?
An umbrella.

A mother, a father, and a son were standing under an umbrella. Which one got wet?
None of them. It wasn't raining.

What disappears when you say its name?
Silence.

What gets wetter the more it dries?
A towel.

How many loaves of bread can you fit in an empty bag?
Just one. After that, it's not empty.

What goes up and down at the same time?
Stairs.

Why can't you starve in a desert?

Because of all the sand which is there.

Which side of a tiger has the most fur?

The outside.

What kind of bow can't be tied?

A rainbow.

What 10-letter word starts with gas?

Automobile.

What happens when you throw a green rock into the Red Sea?

It gets wet.

What kind of animal can go into a bear's cave and come out alive?

A bear.

A man and a horse rode into town. The man stayed two days, then rode out on Tuesday. **What was the horse's name?**

Tuesday.

What's the best way to make pants last?

Just make the shirt and jacket first.

What invention allows you to see through walls?

Windows.

What can you add to a bucket of water to make it lighter?

A hole.

The Sphinx's Riddle

The Sphinx's Riddle is one of the most famous riddles of all time. Can you solve it?

"What goes on four legs in the morning, on two legs at noon, and on three legs in the evening?"

Want to know the answer?

A human!

As babies, humans crawl on hands and knees ("four legs").

Then, we walk on two legs in mid-life ("noon").

Then, we use a walking stick or cane ("three legs") when we get old.

HILARIOUS HINKY PINKY!

A **Hink Pink** is a pair of one-syllable words that rhyme, like "fat cat" or "hot pot."

A kind of paste that holds a sneaker together.
Shoe glue.

A pretend reptile with no legs.
Fake snake.

A large piece of fruit.
Big fig.

A fenced-in area for chickens.
Hen pen.

A rodent's home.
Mouse house.

An icy hammer.
Cool tool.

A **Hinky Pinky** is a pair of two-syllable words that rhyme, like "lizard wizard."

A convenient sweet treat.
Handy candy.

Something to keep a baby cat's paw warm.
Kitten mitten.

A police officer that patrols the dog park.
Pooper trooper.

A tummy that stinks.
Smelly belly.

An inexperienced sweet biscuit.
Rookie cookie.

A wet canine.
Soggy doggy.

A superior cardigan.
Better sweater.

Head-Scratchers and Hink Pinks

What has five fingers but no arm?
A glove.

A person who robs the library.
Book crook.

What has four wheels and flies?
A garbage truck.

A glum father.
Sad dad.

A cool person who recently finished school.
Rad grad.

What month has 28 days?
All of them.

What room has no ceiling, no walls, and no floor?
A mushroom.

The Giant Joke Book for Kids

Knock, Knock! Who's There? Fun!

Illustrations © Shutterstock 2023 Alena Ohneva; Anna Druzhkova; Artem Musaev; HitToon; Kate Kalita; Kwok Design; MyClipArtStore.com; Nadya_Art; Nora Hachio; Olga Utchenko; Orange Vectors; Pushnova; robuart; Rvector; Selin Serhii; Sudowoodo; USBFCO; vectorplus; Yayayoyo

TABLE OF CONTENTS

Know Your Knock-Knocks **56**

Name Games **58**

Number One Knock-Knock Jokes................ **68**

You Animal! **70**

Food Is Funny! **72**

Extra Knock-Knocks! **74**

Keep the Knock-Knocks Coming! **76**

KNOW YOUR KNOCK-KNOCKS

Knock, knock?

Who's there?

A knock-knock joke.

A knock-knock joke who?

A knock-knock joke that's going to make you giggle!

Knock-knock jokes are classic! They've been popular for a long time. Every time you hear a joke start with the famous, "Knock, knock. Who's there?" you know you are about to have some fun. You will probably be surprised with something very silly! And you will probably have a good laugh too! Knock-knock jokes are popular around the world! People find them funny in countries from India to Australia to the United States.

Answer the Joke!

Knock-knocks are a "call and answer" joke. What does that mean? That means there's a person who tells the joke—the caller.

> The caller: *"Knock, knock."*

And then, there's a different person who answers the joke.

> The person who answers: *"Who's there?"*

Two people make the joke even more fun! The person who answers doesn't know the joke. They usually have a good laugh in the end.

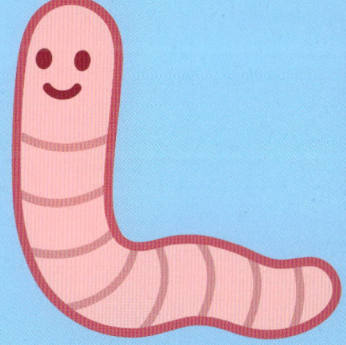

NAME GAMES

Knock, knock.
> Who's there?

Rita.
> Rita who?

Rita joke book and maybe you'll be funny too!

Knock, knock.
> Who's there?

Doris.
> Doris who?

Doris locked. That's why I'm knocking.

Knock, knock.
> Who's there?

Alex.
> Alex who?

Alex-plain later.

Knock, knock.
> Who's there?

Harry.
> Harry who?

Harry up and open the door!

TEE HEE!

Knock, knock.
>Who's there?

Shirley.
>Shirley who?

Shirley you can open the door.

Knock, knock.
>Who's there?

Cher.
>Cher who?

Cher is cold outside!

Knock, knock.
>Who's there?

Leena.
>Leena who?

Leena little closer, and I'll tell you.

History of Knock-Knock Jokes

Knock-knock jokes became very popular in the United States in the 1930s. People loved them so much! Knock-knock jokes were included in songs. People told knock-knock jokes on the radio. Businesses hosted knock-knock joke contests. That's almost 100 years of knock-knock jokes!

Knock, knock.
　　Who's there?
Les.
　　Les who?
Les tell another knock-knock joke!

Knock, knock.
　　Who's there?
Alison.
　　Alison who?
Alison to you if you listen to me.

Knock, knock.
　　Who's there?
Ida.
　　Ida who?
Ida been here sooner, but I got lost.

Knock, knock.
　　Who's there?
Isadore.
　　Isadore who?
Isadore locked?

HA HA!

Knock, knock.
   Who's there?
Gus.
   Gus who?
I give up! Who are you?

Knock, knock.
   Who's there?
Jess.
   Jess who?
Jess open the door already!

Knock, knock.
   Who's there?
Sadie.
   Sadie who?
Sadie magic words, and I'll tell you.

FUNNY FACT

In the 1930s, knock-knock jokes were heard EVERYWHERE. Some people didn't like them. They thought they were annoying and wanted them to go away. But knock-knock jokes are still popular today!

Knock, knock.

> Who's there?

Philip.

> Philip who?

Philip the bathtub a little more.

Knock, knock.

> Who's there?

Dwayne.

> Dwayne who?

Dwayne the bathtub. I'm drowning!

Knock, knock.

> Who's there?

Justin.

> Justin who?

Justin the neighborhood and thought I'd drop by!

FUNNY FACT

National Knock-Knock Joke Day is October 31st. Halloween! Maybe that's because Halloween is the day when we all knock on doors?

Knock, knock.
> Who's there?

Sharon.
> Sharon who?

Sharon your candy sure would be sweet.

Knock, knock.
> Who's there?

Sarah.
> Sarah who?

Sarah doctor in the house?

Knock, knock.
> Who's there?

Amanda.
> Amanda who?

Amanda fix the doorbell's here.

Knock, knock.
> Who's there?

Norma Lee.
> Norma Lee who?

Norma Lee I'd ring the bell, but I think it's broken!

Knock, knock.
　Who's there?
Arthur.
　Arthur who?
Arthur any jokes I don't know?

Knock, knock.
　Who's there?
Colin.
　Colin who?
Colin leave a message after the beep.

Knock, knock.
　Who's there?
Juan.
　Juan who?
Juan to hear some more knock-knock jokes?

Funny Moments in Knock-Knock Joke History!

* Some people think the first knock-knock joke was written by William Shakespeare in the 1600s.

* Knock-knock jokes became popular in other countries around the world by the 1950s.

* Knock-knock jokes were a big part of a comedy TV show in the 1960s called *Laugh-In*. *Laugh-In* was a TV show all about comedy!

Knock, knock.
> Who's there?

Sherwood.
> Sherwood who?

Sherwood like to come inside!

Knock, knock.
> Who's there?

Isabelle.
> Isabelle who?

Isabelle working? Or should I keep knocking?

Knock, knock.
> Who's there?

Howie.
> Howie who?

Good, thanks. How are you?

HEE HEE!

Knock, knock.
> Who's there?

Wilma.
> Wilma who?

Wilma pet elephant fit through the door?

Knock, knock.
> Who's there?

Ben.
> Ben who?

Ben wondering when you'd answer the door.

HEE HEE!

Knock, knock.
> Who's there?

Ken.
> Ken who?

Ken you let me in now?

Knock, knock.
> Who's there?

Luke.
> Luke who?

Luke into my eyes. You're getting very sleepy.

Knock, knock.
> Who's there?

Ivan.
> Ivan who?

Ivan to come inside!

Knock, knock.
> Who's there?

Dewey.
> Dewey who?

Dewey have to keep doing more knock-knock jokes?

Knock, knock.
> Who's there?

Wanda.
> Wanda who?

Wanda go out for a walk?

Knock, knock.
> Who's there?

Anita.
> Anita who?

Anita break from all these knock-knock jokes!

FUNNY FACT

Knock-knock jokes were featured in a 1920s kids' game called "Buff."

In the game, one kid would hit a stick on the ground to make a knocking noise. Then, the kids would tell this joke:

Knock, knock.
> Who's there?

Buff.
> What says "Buff"?

Buff says "Buff" to all his men, and I say "Buff" to you again!

Number One Knock-Knock Jokes

1

Knock, knock.
Who's there?
One.
One who?
One-der why your doorbell doesn't work.

2

Knock, knock.
Who's there?
Two.
Two who?
Don't cry! We'll get your doorbell fixed!

Funny Fact

There are entire books just about knock-knock jokes. Like this one! There are video game-themed knock-knock joke books. There are books with knock-knock jokes about Valentine's Day and Christmas. Can you make up a knock-knock joke about your favorite holiday?

Knock, knock.
> Who's there?

Four.
> Four who?

Four-got my keys again! Let me in!

Knock, knock.
> Who's there?

Eight.
> Eight who?

I eight dinner here last night. Can I come back for dinner tonight?

Knock, knock.
> Who's there?

Ninety.
> Ninety who?

Ninety-night! Sleep tight!

Knock, knock.
> Who's there?

Fascinate.
> Fascinate who?

My coat has nine buttons, but I can only fascinate.

YOU ANIMAL!

Knock, knock.
> Who's there?

Bear.
> Bear who?

Bear with me. My key is stuck.

Knock, knock.
> Who's there?

Owl.
> Owl who?

Owl wipe my feet before I come in.

Knock, knock.
> Who's there?

Beehive.
> Beehive who?

Beehive yourself!

FUNNY FACT

Did you know in many cultures, people knock on wood for good luck?

BAHAHAHA!

Knock, knock.
> Who's there?

Cow says.
> Cow says who?

No, cow says "Moo!"

Knock, knock.
> Who's there?

Panther.
> Panther who?

Panther no pants, I'm going swimming!

Knock, knock.
> Who's there?

Lion.
> Lion who?

Lion is never the answer. Tell the truth!

FOOD IS FUNNY!

Knock, knock.
    Who's there?
Lettuce.
    Lettuce who?
Lettuce in. It's cold outside.

Knock, knock.
    Who's there?
Omelet.
    Omelet who?
Omelet funnier than I look!

Knock, knock.
    Who's there?
Banana.
    Banana who?
Knock, knock.
    Who's there?
Banana.
    Banana who?
Knock, knock.
    Who's there?
Banana.
    Banana who?
Knock, knock.
    Who's there?
Orange.
    Orange who?
Orange you glad I didn't say banana again?

Knock, knock.
　Who's there?
Pizza.
　Pizza who?
Pizza real nice guy!

Knock, knock.
　Who's there?
Butter.
　Butter who?
Butter open the door already!

Knock, knock.
　Who's there?
Juicy.
　Juicy who?
Juicy where I left my keys?

Knock, knock.
　Who's there?
Olive.
　Olive who?
Olive you.

FUNNY FACT

The month of January is named after Janus, the ancient Roman god of doors!

EXTRA KNOCK-KNOCKS!

Knock, knock.
　Who's there?
Little old lady.
　Little old lady who?
I didn't know you could yodel!

FUNNY FACT

This was the first knock-knock joke used in a newspaper in 1934:

Knock, knock.
　Who's there?
Rufus.
　Rufus who?
Rufus the most important part of your house.

Knock, knock.
　Who's there?
Closure.
　Closure who?
Closure mouth when you chew!

HA HA!

Knock, knock.
> Who's there?

Tank.
> Tank who?

You're welcome!

Knock, knock.
> Who's there?

Offer.
> Offer who?

Offer got my key! Let me in!

Knock, knock.
> Who's there?

Canoe.
> Canoe who?

Canoe tell me what time it is?

Knock, knock.
> Who's there?

Water.
> Water who?

Water you doing?

Knock, knock.
> Who's there?

Radio.
> Radio who?

Radio not, here I come!

Knock, knock.
> Who's there?

Senior.
> Senior who?

Senior light on, so I knew you were home.

Knock, knock.
> Who's there?

Woo.
> Woo who?

What are you so excited about?

KEEP THE KNOCK-KNOCKS COMING!

Knock, knock.
> Who's there?

Hutch.
> Hutch who?

Cover your nose when you sneeze!

Knock, knock.
> Who's there?

Snow.
> Snow who?

Snow more knock-knock jokes. I'm tired!

Knock, knock.
> Who's there?

Boo.
> Boo who?

You don't have to cry about it!

Knock, knock.
> Who's there?

Emma.
> Emma who?

Emma makin' you laugh yet?

The Giant Joke Book for Kids

Otter This World

Animal Jokes

Illustrations © Shutterstock 2023 Aleshart16; Alfmaler; brgfx; Butterfly Hunter; dedMazay; Dreamcreation; elza fahrurrozi; graphic-line; Igillustrator; innakreativ; Memo Angeles; natchapohn; Olga Utchenko; Pushnova; Refluo; SaveJungle; Selin Serhii; Shanvood; Spreadthesign; summer studio; sundatoon; Teguh Mujiono; TRONIN ANDREI; vectorplus; vonDUCK; Yayayoyo

TABLE OF CONTENTS

Introduction to Animal Jokes 80

Turtle-y Hilarious! 82

Don't Have a Cow! 86
Jokes about Farm Animals

Jokes on the Wild Side 90

Meows, Barks, and Giggles 92
Jokes about Cats and Dogs

Just Winging It 94
Jokes about Insects, Birds, and More

Foot Stompin' Funny Elephant Jokes 96

Dino-Mite Dinosaur Jokes! 98

Joke-trotter 100
Jokes about Animals around the World

INTRODUCTION
TO ANIMAL JOKES

I am totally koala-fied!

Animals aren't just cute. They can also be really funny. Think about how dogs chase their own tails. Or how some goats faint when they get scared. Or how penguins slide down icy hills on their bellies. So many animals make us giggle!

Do you have any animals at home? Can you think of funny things they do that make you laugh?

Dogs are really funny! But, the kings and queens of animal comedy are cats. In fact, silly cat videos are one of the most popular things on the internet. Of course, we love laughing at silly jokes about other animals too!

Animal names are perfect for puns! Remember, those are jokes that use two words that sound the same but mean different things. Instead of "that's so silly!" wouldn't it be much funnier to say, "that's so seal-y"?

In fact, we're not "lion" that animal puns can be "shrimply" the best!

We're not "kitten"! Now, go "sea otter" for yourself...

TURTLE-Y HILARIOUS

What's the difference between a fish and a piano?
You can't tuna fish.

Why didn't the shrimp want to share?
It was a little shellfish.

If you put three ducks in a carton, what do you get?
A box of quackers.

Where do fish keep their money?
In a riverbank.

TEE HEE!

Where's the best place to see a man-eating fish?

At a seafood restaurant.

What did the lobster say when it went in the pot?

"Boy, am I in hot water!"

Why is it so easy to weigh fish?

Because they come with scales.

Who lends money to fish?

The loan shark.

Giggling Gorillas?

Did you know that some animals laugh? Apes, such as gorillas, and rats are the two types of animals that giggle. Just like us! In experiments, rats will make chirping sounds that scientists think is laughter. It's the same sound they make when they play!

Why are fish so smart?
You usually find them in schools.

What kind of fish can fly?
Angelfish.

What did the worm say to the fisherman?
"Can't we de-bait this?"

How do snails stay so shiny?
With snail polish.

HA HA!

What do frogs like to eat with their hamburgers?
French flies.

How does a fisherman fix a broken hook?
With some tapeworm.

Why couldn't the frog catch the fly?
It was tongue-tied.

What hours do beavers work?
They go gnawing till five.

DON'T HAVE A COW!
JOKES ABOUT FARM ANIMALS

What do you call a pig who plays basketball?
A ball hog.

Why couldn't the pony talk?
Because it was a little hoarse.

Why do cows have bells?
Because their horns are broken.

What do you call a cow with no legs?
Ground beef.

Where do horses go to study?
The neeeigh-borhood library.

What's the most popular game at cow birthday parties?
Moo-sical chairs!

How do farmers count their cows?
With a cow-culator.

Why was the horse such a bad dancer?
It had two left feet.

What do cows do on Friday nights?
Have an udderly good time.

FUNNY FACT

Butterflies taste with their feet! That's TOE-tally cool!

Where do sheep go to study?
The ewe-niversity.

Why did the other animals dislike the goat?
It was always butting in.

How do pigs get to the hospital?
In a ham-bulance.

What's gray and has four legs and a trunk?
A mouse going on vacation.

Why do caterpillars get dressed up?

So they can go to the moth ball.

Why did everyone believe the cow when it lied?

It sounded so bull-lievable.

What's the worst animal to see in your dreams?

A nightmare.

What do you call a rude cow?

Beef jerky.

HEE HEE!

Did You Know?

Did you know people absolutely love cat videos? Who doesn't?

Cats are so silly. They make us laugh. They chase each other around the house. They get tangled up in balls of yarn. And they pounce into paper bags and boxes.

Cats are the most popular stars of YouTube. People love watching them. Cat videos have more than 26 billion views!

JOKES ON THE WILD SIDE

What do you call a deer with no eyes?
No-eyed deer.

Why do pandas have wild parties?
It's always panda-monium.

Remember – sometimes you have to read a joke out loud for it to make sense. Try it here! Pretty funny, right?!

HEE HEE!

What do you call a motionless deer with no eyes?
Still no-eyed deer.

How do you catch a squirrel?
Climb up a tree and act like a nut.

Can giraffes have babies?

No, they have giraffes.

Why did the skunk fill out so many complaint cards?

It was always raising a stink.

What did the leopard say after it ate dinner?

"That really hit the spot!"

Why is it a bad idea to play a game with a big wild cat?

It might be a cheetah.

How can you tell a kangaroo is really nervous?

It gets really jumpy.

FUNNY FACT

The tongues of giant anteaters are two feet long! They must eat f-ANT-astically large dinners!

MEOWS, BARKS, AND GIGGLES
JOKES ABOUT CATS AND DOGS

What do you call a bunch of beagles at the beach?

Hot dogs.

How do you know when it's raining cats and dogs?

When you step in a poodle.

How do you stop a runaway dog?

Just press paws.

FUNNY FACT

Scientists have shown that cats know their own names when called. Sometimes cats just choose to ignore their owners!

What do dogs pack when they go camping?
Their pup tents.

Why did the cat have to go to the dentist?
It ate too many tweets.

What is a cat's favorite color?
Purrrr-ple.

How do cats keep their drinks cold?
With mice cubes.

What kind of dog knows how to tell time?
A watchdog.

Why did the tiger want dogs that couldn't bark?
It loved hush puppies.

JUST WINGING IT
JOKES ABOUT INSECTS, BIRDS, AND MORE

BAHAHAHA!

How do we know that birds are poor?

Because money doesn't grow on trees.

What did the bee say to the flower?

"Hey bud, when do you open?"

Why did the spider move out of its house?

It didn't like its web site.

FUNNY FACT

Slugs have four noses. Smell that to all your friends!

What did the owl say about the goose?

"It doesn't give a hoot!"

Why do hummingbirds hum? Because they don't know the words.

What kind of bugs live on the moon? Lunar-ticks.

What kind of animal makes the best comedian? A mockingbird.

Why do birds fly south for the winter? Because it's too far to walk.

What's better than a talking parrot? A spelling bee.

How do you say goodbye to an owl? "Owl see you later!"

FOOT STOMPIN' FUNNY ELEPHANT JOKES

What time is it when an elephant sits on your fence?
Time to get a new fence.

What do elephants have that nothing else has?
Baby elephants.

What time is it when 10 elephants are chasing you?
Ten after one.

Why are elephants wrinkled?
Have you ever tried to iron one?

Why is an elephant big, gray, and wrinkly?
Because if it were small, white, and fluffy, it would be a bunny.

HA HA!

Why did the elephants go on strike?
They were tired of working for peanuts.

Why can't a herd of elephants get really clean?
Because they never take off their trunks.

What's gray, weighs 2,000 pounds, and has two trunks?
An elephant going on vacation.

Why do elephants have trunks?
Because they don't have glove compartments.

FUNNY FACT

Did you know that a blue whale's tongue weighs more than some elephants? Whale, that's surprising!

DINO-MITE DINOSAUR JOKES!

What's as big as a dinosaur but doesn't weigh anything?
A dinosaur's shadow.

What do you call a dinosaur that walked through the mud?
A brown-toe-saurus.

What kind of dinosaur never gives up?
A try-try-tryceratops.

What's the scariest kind of dinosaur?
A terror-dactyl.

How did dinosaurs knock down trees?
With a dino-saw.

FUNNY FACT

The Stegosaurus was huge! It weighed around 6,000 pounds. But, its brain was about the size of a ping-pong ball!

How do you know when a Stegosaurus is sleeping?
You can hear the dino-snores.

Why did the dinosaur love pancakes?
It was a tri-syrup-tops.

What is a dinosaur's favorite instrument?
A trombone.

What do dinosaurs say when they shake hands?
Pleased to eat you.

What do you call a dinosaur in a china shop?
Tyrannosaurus wrecks.

What's louder than a dinosaur?
A herd of dinosaurs.

JOKE-TROTTER: JOKES ABOUT ANIMALS AROUND THE WORLD

Why do anteaters eat ants?
Because uncles give them tummy aches.

What do you call seagulls that live by the bay?
Bagels.

What's a rabbit's favorite kind of music?
Hip-hop.

Can an elephant jump higher than a house?
Of course! A house can't jump at all!

What's invisible and smells like bananas?
Monkey burps.

Why are leopards bad at hide and seek?
They're always spotted.

HEE HEE!

TEE HEE!

HA HA!

BA HA HA HA!

HEE HEE!

BA HA HA HA!

HEE HEE!

TEE HEE!

HA HA!

HEE HEE!